BIOGRAPHIES

MARTIN LUTHER KING JR.
PREACHER, FREEDOM FIGHTER, PEACEMAKER

Written by Pamela Hill Nettleton
Illustrated by Garry Nichols

Special thanks to our advisers for their expertise:

Gregory L. Kaster, Ph.D., Chair, Department of History
Gustavus Adolphus College, St. Peter, Minnesota

Susan Kesselring, M.A., Literacy Educator
Rosemount–Apple Valley–Eagan (Minnesota) School District

PICTURE WINDOW BOOKS
MINNEAPOLIS, MINNESOTA

Managing Editor: Bob Temple
Creative Director: Terri Foley
Editor: Peggy Henrikson
Editorial Adviser: Andrea Cascardi
Copy Editor: Laurie Kahn
Prototype: Claire Berge
Page production: The Design Lab
The illustrations in this book were rendered digitally.

PICTURE WINDOW BOOKS
5115 Excelsior Boulevard
Suite 232
Minneapolis, MN 55416
1-877-845-8392
www.picturewindowbooks.com

Printed in the United States of America.

Library of Congress Cataloging-in-Publication Data
Nettleton, Pamela Hill.
Martin Luther King, Jr. : preacher, freedom fighter, peacemaker / written by Pamela Hill
Nettleton ; illustrated by Garry Nichols.
p. cm. – (Biographies)
Summary: A brief biography that highlights some important events in the life of the man
who won a Nobel Peace Prize for his nonviolent support of civil rights.
Includes bibliographical references (p.) and index.
ISBN 1-4048-0188-X
1. King, Martin Luther, Jr., 1929–1968–Juvenile literature. 2. African Americans–
Biography–Juvenile literature. 3. Civil rights workers–United States–Biography–
Juvenile literature. 4. Baptists–United States–Clergy–Biography–Juvenile literature.
5. African Americans–Civil rights–History–20th century–Juvenile literature. [1. King,
Martin Luther, Jr., 1929–1968. 2. Civil rights workers. 3. Clergy. 4. Civil rights move-
ments–History. 5. African Americans–Biography.] I. Nichols, Garry, 1958– ill. II. Title.
E185.97.K5 N425 2003
323′.092–dc21   2003004122

Some people have lives that touch many others. They do great things that we remember even after they are gone. Martin Luther King Jr. was one of those people.

Martin fought for justice and peace among black people and white people. He fought with words and ideas. He fought with strong but peaceful actions. He helped bring about many changes for the better.

This is Martin's story.

Martin Luther King Jr. was born in 1929 in Atlanta, Georgia. His father was a minister, and his mother was a teacher.

Martin loved books and words. One day, he heard a man make a good speech. Martin told his mother that someday *he* was going to use big words like that.

When Martin was six years old, he went to a school just for black children. His white friends had their own school. He missed them.

Martin learned that laws kept black people and white people apart. Angry feelings kept people apart, too.

Martin's mother told him he was as good as anyone. She said he should feel like he *was* somebody, even when he was treated badly.

Martin was a good student. He was so smart, he started college when he was only 15 years old. In graduate school, Martin met Coretta Scott. He married her, and they moved to Montgomery, Alabama.

Martin and his wife, Coretta, had four children. Coretta studied music and was a singer.

Martin became a minister at a church in Montgomery.
He loved to talk, so he made a good preacher.

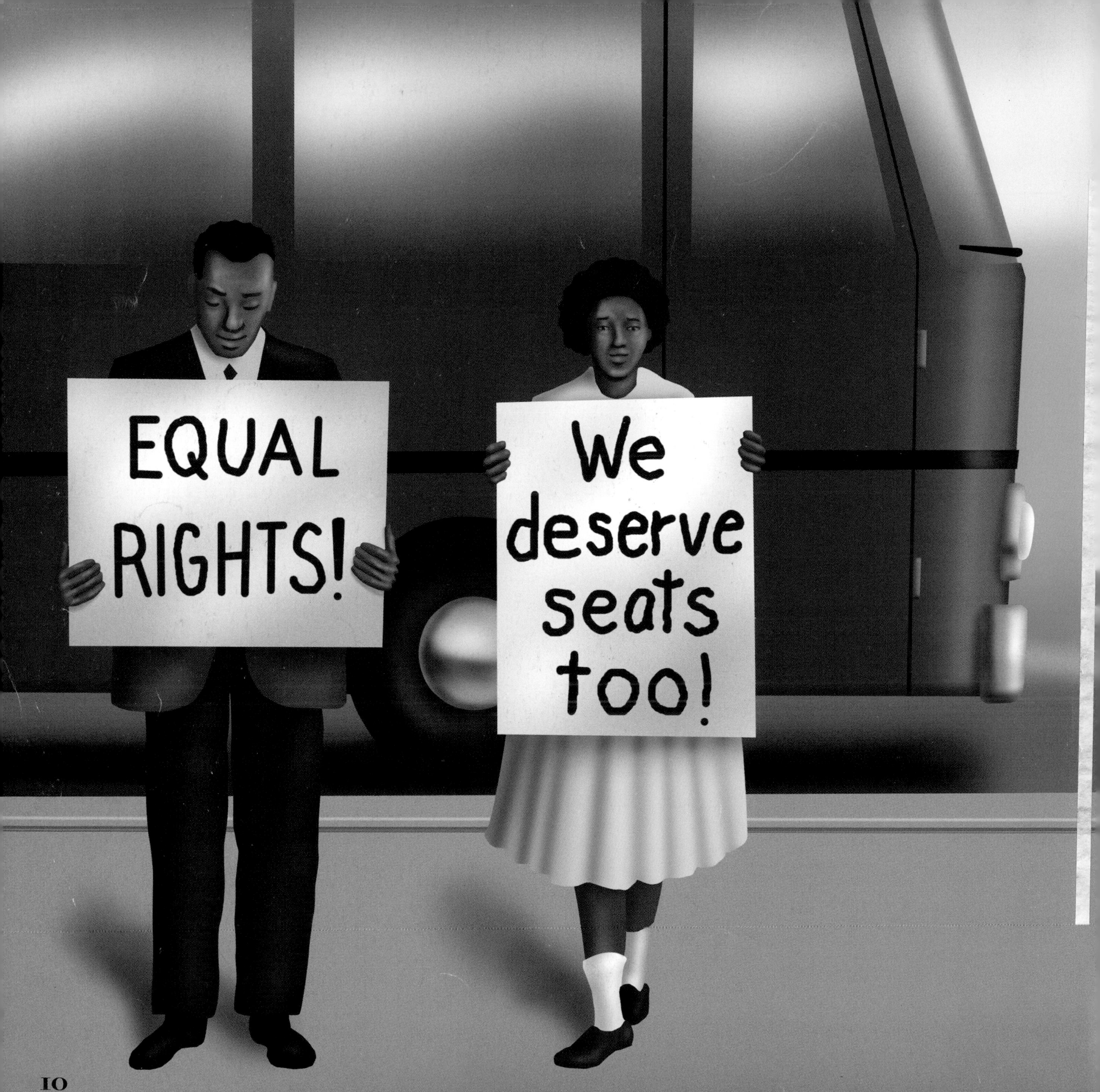
EQUAL
RIGHTS!
We
deserve
seats
too!

One day in 1955, a bus driver asked a black woman named Rosa Parks to give up her seat to a white person. This was the law, but Rosa was tired. She said no, and she was arrested.

Martin and other black leaders in Montgomery asked people to stop riding buses until the law changed. This bus boycott hurt the bus company's business and made the whole country notice. Finally, the government changed the unfair laws.

BUS STOP

Not all the laws changed, though. Some restaurants were still for white people only. Some hotels did not let black people stay there.

Martin asked blacks and whites to go to these places and just sit together. This was called a sit-in. Sometimes the people were arrested for doing this.

Whites Only

Martin was arrested 30 times.
All he did was go where black
people were not supposed to go.

Martin told black people not to fight with anger.
He told them to talk, sit, or march in peace.

JUSTICE

EQUALITY FOR ALL

VOTING IS OUR RIGHT

He used his own big words to talk about big ideas. His words were strong and brave. Martin changed people's minds and hearts and lives for the better.

Some people did not like it when Martin and other black people spoke out against the old laws. They bombed Martin's home and his church.

In 1963, Martin helped to lead more than 200,000 people in a march to Washington, D.C. The marchers wanted black people to be treated the same as white people. This famous event became known as the March on Washington.

"I have a dream!" Martin told a huge crowd at the Lincoln Memorial. He dreamed that people would stop being angry and afraid. He dreamed that his children would not be judged by the color of their skin but by who they were.

Martin Luther King Jr. won many awards. In 1964, he was the youngest person ever to win the Nobel Peace Prize.

Some of Martin's dreams came true.
In 1964, President Lyndon Johnson
signed a new law. The law said
all Americans must be treated the same.

Martin kept working to make life better
for all people. He talked about helping
poor people get enough to eat and find jobs.
He spoke out against Americans going
to war in Vietnam.

Some people did not understand. They were angry at Martin for his ideas. On April 4, 1968, Martin was shot and killed. Many people were very sad. They missed Martin and his wise words.

But they did not forget his powerful ideas about peace and fairness. Martin and his ideas are honored on a special holiday every year. It is a day of remembering for the whole country.

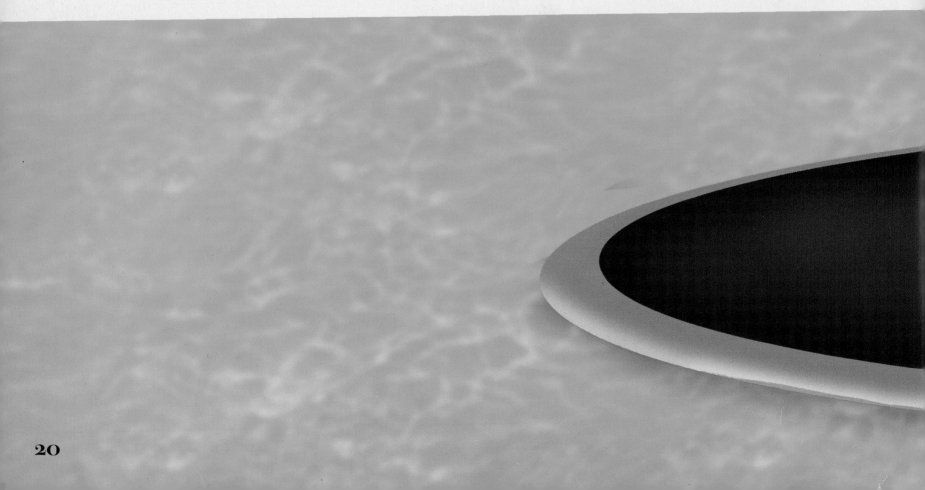

Martin Luther King Jr. Day is
the third Monday in January.

The Life of Martin Luther King Jr.

1929   Born on January 15 in Atlanta, Georgia

1948   Graduated from Morehouse College.
Became a Baptist minister at age 19.

1953   Married Coretta Scott and moved to Montgomery, Alabama

1955–56   Led bus boycott after Rosa Parks was arrested.
U.S. Supreme Court ruled that blacks and whites
have the same rights on buses.

1957   Formed a group called the Southern Christian Leadership
Conference to fight for equal rights for black people.
In this year alone, Martin made 208 speeches.

1963   Led the March on Washington and gave his
"I Have a Dream" speech

1964   Attended signing of the Civil Rights Act of 1964
at the White House.
Was awarded the Nobel Peace Prize.

1968   Was shot and killed in Memphis, Tennessee

1986   The first Martin Luther King Jr. Day was observed
as a national holiday on January 20.

Did You Know?

- Martin entered college when he was only 15 because he skipped grades 9 and 12.

- When Martin was born, he was named Michael after his father. When Martin was young, his father changed both their names to Martin Luther. Martin was called M.L. by his family.

- Martin's father, grandfather, great-grandfather, brother, and uncle were all ministers, too.

- Martin and his father were ministers together in the same church.

- Martin didn't start out wanting to be a minister. At first, he thought about being a doctor or lawyer. He ended up earning a high degree in religion, so people called him Dr. King. But he was a doctor of religion, not a doctor of medicine.

- Three generations of Kings attended Morehouse College.

Glossary

arrest (uh-REST)—to stop and hold someone for doing something against the law

award (uh-WARD)—a prize; an official honor

boycott (BOI-kot)—to refuse to buy things from a company or use its services to force it to change its ways. Martin asked people to boycott the bus company.

justice (JUHSS-tiss)—fairness

minister (MIN-uh-stur)—a person who leads church services and ceremonies

preacher (PREE-chur)—a person who gives religious speeches

Supreme Court (suh-PREEM KORT)—the most powerful court in the United States

To Learn More

At the Library

Adler, David A. *A Picture Book of Martin Luther King, Jr.* New York: Holiday House, 1989.

Farris, Christine King. *My Brother Martin.* New York: Simon & Schuster Books for Young Readers, 2002.

Rappaport, Doreen. *Martin's Big Words: The Life of Dr. Martin Luther King, Jr.* New York: Hyperion Books for Children, 2001.

Ringgold, Faith. *My Dream of Martin Luther King.* New York: Crown, 1995.

Schaefer, Lola M. *Martin Luther King, Jr.* Mankato, Minn.: Pebble Books/Capstone Press, 1999.

On the Web

LIFE CLASSIC IMAGES: MLK JR.

See photos of Martin and his family from Life magazine
http://www.life.com/Life/mlk/mlkpics.html

EDUCATION PLANET: MARTIN LUTHER KING, JR.

For many links and resources for children's activities regarding Martin Luther King Jr.
http://www.educationplanet.com/articles/mlk.html#child

FACT HOUND

Fact Hound offers a safe, fun way to find Web sites related to this book. All of the sites on Fact Hound have been researched by our staff.
http://www.facthound.com
1. Visit the Fact Hound home page.
2. Enter a search word related to this book, or type in this special code: 140480188X.
3. Click on the FETCH IT button.
Your trusty Fact Hound will fetch the best sites for you!

On a Trip

NATIONAL PARK SERVICE:
MARTIN LUTHER KING JR.—NATIONAL HISTORIC SITE
450 Auburn Avenue, NE
Atlanta, GA 30312-1525
(404) 331-6922
http://www.nps.gov/malu
Visit the places where Dr. King was born, where he worked and worshiped, and where he was buried.
Kids between the ages of 9 and 12 can inquire about the Junior Ranger Program of activities and principles.

Index